Prosecco is good for you

A comical collection of quotes for prosecco princesses

ISBN: 978-1-912155-89-7

Created by Reckless Indiscretions
Images under license from Shuttertock

BELL & MACKENZIE
www.bellmackenzie.com

LAUGHTER
IS THE BEST
MEDICINE...
IF YOU CAN'T FIND THE
PROSECCO

This house runs on love, laughter and prosecco

Order dessert

Drink prosecco

Love life

There comes a time

in every woman's life

when the

only thing

that will help is

PROSECCO

My head says to go the gym
My heart says drink more
prosecco

PROSECCO MADE ME DO IT

IT'S TIME TO DRINK
PROSECCO
& DANCE
ON THE TABLE

prosecco

is always the answer

If people were wine

she was prosecco

...bubbly & intoxicating

Oops! I bought

PROSECCO

instead of

~~milk~~

again

Prosecco
is how classy girls get wasted

A BANANA
IS 105 CALORIES
A GLASS OF
PROSECCO IS 80
CHOOSE WISELY

PROSECCO
IS FOR LIFE
NOT JUST
FOR
CHRISTMAS

Do you know what rhymes with Friday?

prosecco

Anything is possible with a little lipstick and prosecco

If you have to ask
if it's too early to drink

prosecco

you're an

AMATEUR

A woman cannot survive on prosecco alone
She also needs shoes

THERE IS ONLY ONE THING BETTER THAN
A GLASS OF PROSECCO..
A BOTTLE

TOO MUCH
OF ANYTHING IS
BAD
BUT TOO MUCH
PROSECCO
IS JUST RIGHT

Every woman

*deserves orange blossom
in her hair*

love

in her heart &

prosecco

in her hand

*Have a little faith
and if that doesn't
work out have a lot
of prosecco*

Prosecco
princesses
make the best
GIRLFRIENDS

§ Move over coffee
Today is a job for prosecco §

PROSECCO
IS LIKE DUCT TAPE
IT FIXES
EVERYTHING

DON'T TELL ME YOU

MISS ME

TELL ME YOU'RE OUTSIDE WITH

PROSECCO

People who think

I'm difficult to buy

for obviously don't

know where to buy

prosecco

Start the day

with a smile

Finish it with

prosecco

LIFE
ISN'T ALWAYS
ponies

&

prosecco

BUT IT SHOULD BE

I only drink prosecco on two occasions...
When I am in love and when I'm not

IN VICTORY
YOU DESERVE PROSECCO
IN DEFEAT
YOU NEED IT

PROSECCO
IS APPROPRIATE
FOR BREAKFAST, LUNCH
OR DINNER

Either give me more

prosecco

or leave me alone

Prosecco is one of the elegant extras in life

If life brings you
troubles

drink some

prosecco

then your problems will just be
BUBBLES

Prosecco is the anesthesia by
which we endure the operation
of life

BRUNCH
WITHOUT PROSECCO
IS JUST A SAD
BREAKFAST

YOU
WERE MY
CUP OF TEA
BUT NOW I DRINK PROSECCO

Tick Tock

it's

prosecco

O'clock

Friends don't let friends drink prosecco alone

I make
prosecco

disappear

What's your

SUPERPOWER?

§ Friends bring happiness
Best friends bring prosecco §

SAVE WATER
DRINK
PROSECCO

TONIGHT'S FORECAST IS

99%

CHANCE OF

PROSECCO

One prosecco
Two prosecco
Three prosecco
Floor

*Silly girl...
There's no such
thing as too much
prosecco*

Keep
calm
& drink
PROSECCO

"I don't really fancy prosecco"
(Said no one. Ever)

YOU
DESERVE
PROSECCO

WHETHER YOUR GLASS IS

HALF EMPTY OR

HALF FULL

THERE IS ALWAYS ROOM FOR MORE

PROSECCO

"Trust me you can dance"

...said prosecco

Prosecco is my

spirit animal

I only drink
prosecco
on days

ending in

' Y '

§ I put the 'pro' in prosecco §

A PARTY WITHOUT PROSECCO IS JUST A MEETING

GOOD THINGS
HAPPEN TO THOSE
WHO DRINK
PROSECCO

We're a bit like

prosecco

you and me

Classy, bubbly and

often drunk at parties

Gluten Free
Dairy Free
Fat Free
I love this prosecco diet

Is there a more pleasing sound in the world than a _cork_ popping?

HELL NO!

§ May you never outgrow bubbles §

THIS PROSECCO IS MAKING ME AWESOME!

THE ANSWER
MAY NOT
LIE AT THE
BOTTOM OF A BOTTLE OF
PROSECCO
BUT WE SHOULD AT LEAST CHECK

Of course size matters

No one wants a

small glass of

prosecco

You don't always

need a plan

Sometimes you just

need prosecco

www.ingramcontent.com/pod-product-compliance
LIghtning Source LLC
Chambersburg PA
CBHW071637040426
42452CB00009B/1674